Introduction

Are you happy? Chances are, if you've found your way to this journal, the answer to that question has become complicated. Just know, whatever you're going through—no matter how difficult—things can get better. You're a good person with a kind heart, and you deserve a life filled with immense joy.

In this journal, I'll introduce you to the tools I've used to change my own life. My path may not work for you; I'm not a self-help guru, therapist, or coach —I'm just someone who's been through some things and found a path that worked for me.

My personal story includes addiction, depression, and anxiety, but I believe these tools can be adapted to fit your unique situation. Use all of them or simply cherry-pick the ones that resonate with you. There are many paths to recovery, but what matters most is that you choose to walk one, rather than staying on the one you're currently on. Let's get it!

Ben Fisher

The Tool Box

The tools I used to change my life

- ☑ **Just Admit It**

- ☑ **Finding Your People**

- ☑ **Finding Your Passion**

- ☑ **Attitude of Gratitude**

- ☑ **Mindful Mindfulness**

- ☑ **K.I.N.D.**
  Kindness Is Now Deliberate

- ☑ **The God of Your Understanding**

- ☑ **Variable In = Variable Out**

- ☑ **Stop Playing the Victim**

Learn more about the author

benfisherinspires.com🔍

Tool #1
Just Admit It

You can't fix a problem unless you first admit you have one. This idea is foundational not just to self-improvement but to the entire process of recovery. In the Big Book (Alcoholics Anonymous), the first step says, "We admitted we were powerless over alcohol—that our lives had become unmanageable." Now, try placing brackets around the word (alcohol) and swapping it out with whatever it is that you're facing. Whether it's anger, control issues, negative self-talk, or even avoidance, naming the problem is a crucial first step.

"When we are too proud to admit our mistakes, we often lose something that is utterly more important than our useless pride."
— Jocelyn Soriano

Humans have this intense urge to be right—it's in our DNA. We're all led by ego to some extent. For some of us, that voice of pride is a constant companion, defending our actions, explaining away our mistakes, and making excuses for why we haven't yet admitted what's wrong. But if we're honest, sometimes we lose sight of what's most important because we're busy holding on to the need to "be right." I love this other quote that captures it perfectly: "It gets lonely when you think you know everything."

That isolation? It's usually because we refuse to let down our guard and admit our missteps. This is one of those rare tools that's non-negotiable. Whatever your issue is, it's not going to get better unless you admit it. So, let's look at some ways to practically bring this idea into our lives.

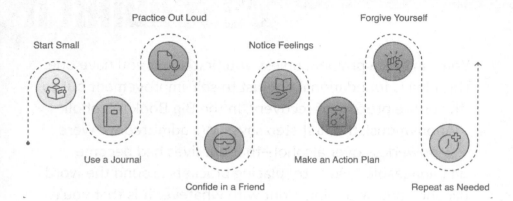

Steps to Implement "Just Admit It

Start Small · Practice Out Loud · Notice Feelings · Forgive Yourself

Use a Journal · Confide in a Friend · Make an Action Plan · Repeat as Needed

Start Small

If admitting a big issue feels intimidating, start with something smaller. Maybe it's a daily habit you've been avoiding, like always being a few minutes late. Try admitting to yourself that being late causes stress and affects others, and commit to taking steps to change it. Practicing with small admissions builds your "admission muscle," making it easier to tackle bigger things over time.

Use a Journal as Your Confession Booth

One of the best places to admit things is to yourself. Grab a journal and make it a safe, no-judgment zone. Write out, "Today, I admit that..." and fill in the blank. Don't overthink it. This could be a behavior, a feeling, or even a fear that you know is affecting your life. Seeing it written down helps you face it honestly, and over time, it becomes less scary.

Practice Out Loud

Sometimes, speaking an admission out loud—especially to yourself—brings a powerful shift. Look in the mirror, take a deep breath, and say, "I admit that ____ is a problem in my life." It may feel awkward, but saying it out loud makes it feel real. It's like telling a friend, even if that friend is yourself. Try this every day until it feels less charged, then consider talking with someone you trust.

Confide in a Trustworthy Friend or Mentor

If you're comfortable, choose someone who's walked a similar path, or just someone you trust. You don't have to share everything; even a simple, "I've been struggling with ___, and I want to work on it" can feel like a huge step forward. Remember, you don't need someone to fix it for you. Just saying it aloud can open up space for progress.

Notice the Feelings That Come Up

Admission brings up all kinds of emotions—embarrassment, regret, even relief. Sit with these feelings without pushing them away or trying to explain them. This is part of the process, and it's okay to feel whatever comes up. Try to accept that these feelings are normal. They'll come and go, and the more you sit with them, the easier it gets.

Make an Action Plan

Once you've admitted what's going on, decide on one small thing you can do to start shifting it. For example, if you've admitted that you avoid conflict at all costs, commit to speaking up in just one conversation this week. You don't need to solve the entire issue overnight. Just knowing the problem is real allows you to start taking action, one step at a time.

Forgive Yourself for Waiting This Long

Admitting something can bring a lot of self-criticism. You might wonder why it took you so long, or feel embarrassed for holding onto it. That's normal. But remember, none of us are perfect. Forgive yourself for the delay and thank yourself for finally being willing to see it. This act of self-kindness is a powerful part of making real change.

Repeat as Needed

Admission isn't a "one and done" kind of thing. Some issues will take time and will need you to re-acknowledge them. That's okay. The courage to admit will get stronger with practice, and each time you're honest with yourself, you're building a solid foundation for real growth.

Journaling Your Experience with "Just Admit It"

Take a moment to reflect on this lesson by journaling about your experience. Use your journal as a safe space to explore what admitting your challenges feels like for you. Don't worry about finding the "right" words—just let your thoughts flow. Remember, there's no judgment here. This is about giving yourself the freedom to be honest, even if it's uncomfortable. Writing can help you see your thoughts more clearly, and it's a powerful step toward growth.

What is one issue, big or small, that you know you need to admit to yourself? Write about why it feels difficult to admit it.

How has avoiding this problem affected your life or your relationships? Be as specific as you can.

What emotions come up when you think about admitting this issue? What do those emotions tell you?

What is one small action you could take to start
addressing this issue? Write about how you could take
this step and what it might feel like.

If you were speaking to a trusted friend or mentor about this, what would you want to tell them? How might they respond?

What's one thing you could forgive yourself for regarding this issue? Why is self-forgiveness important in this process?

_____

_____

_____

_____

_____

_____

_____

_____

_____

_____

_____

_____

_____

_____

How does it feel to write about these things? Do you notice any sense of relief, fear, or hope? Explore these feelings.

Tool #2
Finding Your People

Let's be real: isolation can be deadly. Trying to make big life changes completely alone is like climbing a mountain without ropes—possible, maybe, but so much harder and riskier. To grow, to heal, and to thrive, you need the right people around you. For me, finding those people meant walking into a 12-step recovery meeting, which was uncomfortable at first. But sometimes, to find what we need, we have to step out of our comfort zones. Whether it's a recovery group, a church, a new club, or even bingo night, the important thing is to find a group of people who understand you and where you're coming from.

Going to A.A., cliché as it might sound, saved my life. It became the "secret sauce" that held everything together. To give you some context, I'd already gone through both outpatient and inpatient treatment—spent thousands of dollars, fell flat on my face, and honestly, I'm still a little sour about it. But I'm not saying treatment doesn't work. It does for most people. But at that point in my life, it wasn't doing the trick for me. I was still struggling, still lost.

Joining A.A. meetings gave me a lifeline. At first, I went religiously, attending at least three times a week. But about a year into it, I found myself daydreaming in the middle of meetings, wondering what else I could be doing with my time. It felt stagnant, and I needed something more to keep my recovery alive. Around this time, a family friend suggested I join him in learning how to build guitars. That offer became a turning point. I went for it, and it eventually led to the creation of A String of Hope, which has been deeply meaningful in my life. Through that experience, I met some of my closest friends—people who understand me, support me, and hold me accountable.

Finding that community of like-minded people changed everything. So even though I eventually started attending fewer meetings, I stayed connected to people who "get it" and who would call me out if I strayed too far off track. You see, even though I'm an introvert (yes, surprisingly, I am), I still need that tight-knit network around me to stay grounded.

Why Finding Your People Matters

Supportive community is more than just a safety net—it's a source of growth, strength, and resilience. This is why I believe in Joy Academy so deeply. It's a space where people come together who are seeking similar things. They're possibly struggling with similar challenges or—better yet—are a few steps ahead and can show you the way forward. Connecting with people who are on a similar journey, or who have overcome the same obstacles, can help make the path less lonely and the challenges feel more manageable.

There's this incredible power in connection, and that power can pull you through some of your toughest days. Isolation, on the other hand, has a way of magnifying every struggle and making every fear seem more overwhelming. Without community, it's easy to get lost in the echo chamber of your mind, where doubts and negative thoughts have room to grow unchecked. So, yes, finding your people might mean doing things that feel uncomfortable at first, but trust me, the discomfort is worth it.

Practical Ways to Find Your People

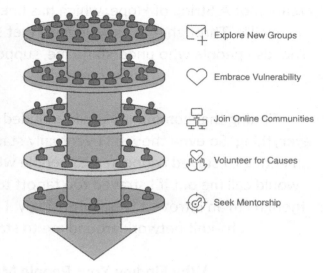

Explore New Groups

Embrace Vulnerability

Join Online Communities

Volunteer for Causes

Seek Mentorship

Identify Your Values and Interests

Reflect on what matters most to you or what you're passionate about. If you're in recovery, maybe it's finding a support group where people share similar experiences. If you're searching for purpose, you could explore classes, workshops, or volunteer opportunities that resonate with your interests. Knowing what you value will guide you toward the right community.

Try New Groups and Stay Open

This can be tough if you're more introverted or if social situations feel intimidating, but try to approach new groups with an open mind. Maybe it's a church group, a creative workshop, or even a community sports league. Don't dismiss options that seem a bit outside your usual zone. The right group for you might be somewhere unexpected.

Embrace Vulnerability

Finding your people isn't just about showing up; it's about letting others see the real you. Be open about what you're going through, even if it feels uncomfortable. Authenticity draws others toward you, especially those who can relate to what you're facing.

Join Online Communities

If in-person connection feels challenging, especially at first, online communities can be a great starting place. Look for spaces that align with your journey. This could be a recovery forum, a self-improvement group, or even a creative hobby community. Online connections can build real friendships and lead to future in-person support networks.

Get Involved in Causes You Care About

Sometimes, the best connections happen when you're focused on a shared purpose. Volunteering or engaging in a cause you believe in can naturally introduce you to people who share your values and passions. This mutual purpose gives you something meaningful to bond over right from the start.

Seek Out a Mentor or Peer Support

If possible, find someone who's a few steps ahead on a similar path. This could be a mentor or a peer who's been through what you're going through. They don't have to have all the answers; just having someone who understands the journey can make a huge difference.

Be Patient

Finding a solid community doesn't always happen right away. It may take time, a few tries, and maybe some trial and error before you meet the people who genuinely support you. Stick with it and trust that the right people will come along.

The Risk of Isolation and the Power of Connection

Never underestimate the harm isolation can bring. Without connection, even small problems can feel massive, and feelings of loneliness can start to feel endless. On the flip side, don't underestimate the strength that comes from sharing your life with others. Surrounding yourself with the right people can provide a sense of belonging and hope that is priceless, especially on days when you feel like giving up.

The people you connect with on this journey become your anchor. They'll understand what others can't, they'll hold you accountable, and they'll remind you that you're not alone. Finding your people isn't just a nice-to-have; it's a lifeline, a reminder that your struggles are shared, and that your victories are celebrated.

So take a deep breath and make the effort. Join the group, attend the meeting, show up, and keep showing up. If you can find your people, you can find the courage to keep moving forward. Let's get out there.

Journaling Your Experience with "Finding Your People"

Reflecting on your journey to find connection can be a powerful experience. Use your journal to explore your thoughts and feelings about community, vulnerability, and the steps you've taken—or could take—to find your people. Writing about this process can help you uncover what's holding you back, what you truly need, and how connection could transform your life. Let your journal be a space to dream about the relationships you want to cultivate and to process the fears or doubts that arise.

Who are the "right people" for you? Describe the kind
of community or relationships you want in your life.
What qualities do these people have?

_____

_____

_____

_____

_____

_____

_____

_____

_____

_____

_____

_____

_____

_____

_____

_____

_____

Have you ever experienced the power of a supportive community? What did it feel like, and how did it impact you?

What fears or hesitations come up when you think about stepping out to find your people? Write about where these feelings might come from.

What interests or passions could guide you toward a community of like-minded people? How might you explore these interests in a group setting?

How do you currently cope with feelings of isolation?
Are these strategies helping you. or could they be
replaced with more meaningful connections?

What's one small step you could take this week to connect with others? Write about how this step feels —exciting, scary, or something else—and why.

_____

_____

_____

_____

_____

_____

_____

_____

_____

_____

_____

_____

_____

_____

Think about someone in your life who has supported you in the past. What made their support meaningful. and how could you find or offer that in a new community?

_____

_____

_____

_____

_____

_____

_____

_____

_____

_____

_____

_____

_____

_____

How would your life change if you had a strong, supportive community around you? Visualize this and write about how it makes you feel.

_____

_____

_____

_____

_____

_____

_____

_____

_____

_____

_____

_____

_____

_____

_____

_____

_____

_____

Take time to revisit these questions as you continue this journey. Finding your people isn't just about external action—it's also about understanding your own needs, desires, and the courage it takes to reach out.

Finding Your New (Healthy) Addiction

You'll often hear people say things like, "Addiction is not a choice. Choosing to pick up, choosing to take that first drink— that's a choice. But addiction itself is a disease." Now, some people push back against the idea of addiction as a disease, and honestly, I don't get why it's even a debate. Addiction is the only disease that carries this particular stigma. You wouldn't look at someone with diabetes and say, "Why don't you just choose not to have diabetes?" even if poor choices may have contributed. At the end of the day, millions of people suffer from addiction. It doesn't matter what we call it —the fact is, it's real and it's insidious.

The truth is, if you're an addict or alcoholic like me, you'll probably spend your life being addicted to something. For years, I was just swapping one unhealthy addiction for another. But during my guitar-building process, I had a revelation: what if I could use my tendency to obsess as a superpower? When I dive into something, I go all in. I don't just dabble—I become consumed, obsessed. And because of that, I work hard, I stay focused, and I don't stop until I reach my goal. It turns out that this obsessive drive—my biggest flaw—is also my greatest strength. Who would've thought, right? All those years, I was leaving out the most important part of the puzzle. And that missing piece? Choosing an obsession that didn't actively try to kill me.

When I finally started filling my time with obsessions that were good for me, my life began to change in ways I hadn't imagined. It started with A.A., then shifted to guitar building, and then to my nonprofit, A String of Hope. Since then, I've had plenty of other "micro-obsessions" along the way: building a tiny house, getting into real estate investing, learning video editing, growing vegetables hydroponically— you get the picture. Each one kept me engaged, moving forward, and, most importantly, out of harm's way.

> "Idle hands are the devil's playthings."
> — Benjamin Franklin

Let me tell you, that quote could have been written just for me. I mentioned earlier that getting bored and antsy is dangerous territory, and I meant it. I've always been a do-er; I like to stay busy, and I need constant stimulation. Having ADHD means I crave action, and if things get too stagnant, I can feel panic rising in my chest. So instead of trying to fight this tendency, I made a shift: I stopped trying to beat addiction itself and instead learned to use it as a tool. It's a fine line, no doubt—a line I'm still learning to walk. But one thing I know for certain: I am an addict at heart.

How to Find Your New (Healthy) Addiction

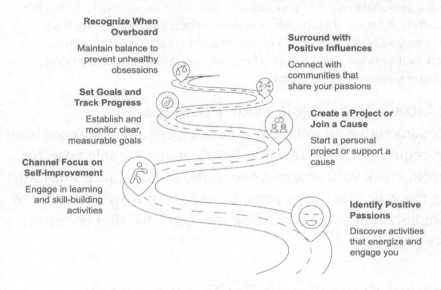

Recognize When Overboard
Maintain balance to prevent unhealthy obsessions

Set Goals and Track Progress
Establish and monitor clear, measurable goals

Channel Focus on Self-Improvement
Engage in learning and skill-building activities

Surround with Positive Influences
Connect with communities that share your passions

Create a Project or Join a Cause
Start a personal project or support a cause

Identify Positive Passions
Discover activities that energize and engage you

Identify Positive Passions and Interests

Think about the activities that make you feel alive. If you don't know yet, start exploring. Experiment with creative projects, physical activities, or even intellectual pursuits. Your new addiction should be something that energizes you and brings you a sense of purpose. Look for things that can challenge and engage you long-term.

Channel Your Focus on Self-Improvement

Learning new skills or working on self-improvement is an incredible way to channel addictive tendencies. Take classes, read books, practice something that requires time and dedication, whether that's fitness, art, cooking, or even a side business. This way, you're not just filling time—you're building skills and confidence.

Create a Project or Join a Cause

Having a personal project or supporting a cause can be deeply fulfilling. For me, starting A String of Hope became that anchor. Find something that matters to you. Volunteer, join a cause, or even create something from scratch. Not only will this keep you busy, but you'll also be contributing something meaningful to the world.

Set Goals and Track Your Progress

Addictions thrive on instant gratification, but a healthy obsession often requires delayed rewards. Set clear, measurable goals for yourself. Track your progress over time, and celebrate small wins along the way. This keeps you engaged and gives you a sense of accomplishment without needing the "quick fix" that unhealthy habits provide.

Surround Yourself with Positive Influences

Spending time with people who share similar interests will motivate you to stick with your healthy obsessions. Join a club, attend a group, or find an online community where you can share your passion and be around others who are on the same path. You don't have to do this alone.

Recognize When You're Going Overboard

This is important. Even healthy obsessions can cross the line into unhealthy territory. Keep an eye on your balance. If one interest starts taking over to the point that you're ignoring everything else, check in with yourself and reset if needed. A healthy addiction should add to your life, not replace it.

Embrace "Micro-Obsessions"

Sometimes, you may not need one big obsession; instead, you could thrive on a series of smaller ones. "Micro-obsessions" can keep you interested and energized without requiring long-term commitment. This could be anything from learning a new recipe, trying out a DIY project, or researching a new hobby in-depth just for the joy of it. Keep it light, and allow yourself the freedom to shift when the interest fades.

Turn Mundane Tasks into Purposeful Routines

Not every healthy obsession needs to be glamorous. Even ordinary routines like cleaning, organizing, or cooking can become satisfying rituals when approached with focus and purpose. By turning mundane activities into purposeful routines, you're able to channel your energy into something simple and constructive.

Using Addiction as a Tool, Not a Trap

Finding a healthy addiction doesn't mean you're free of challenges, but it does mean you're learning to direct your energy and obsessiveness in a way that works for you rather than against you. Over time, you'll develop a skill set and mindset that allows you to handle boredom, restlessness, and the need for stimulation without falling back into destructive habits. When you use your addiction as a tool, you're transforming what might have once been your downfall into a source of strength.

I'm not saying it's easy or that I have it all figured out. But I do know that choosing healthy obsessions has saved my life in countless ways. By directing your energy toward something positive, you can build the life you want, one day and one healthy obsession at a time. Let's get started.

Journaling Your Experience with "Using Addiction as a Tool"

Exploring the concept of channeling addictive tendencies into positive outlets can be deeply empowering. Use your journal to reflect on how this idea resonates with you and to identify ways you might use your energy for good. Writing about your experiences and emotions can help clarify what drives your habits, how they've impacted your life, and how you might redirect them into healthier pursuits. Be honest and open with yourself—this process is about understanding, not judgment.

What are some habits or tendencies in your life that you think stem from an "addictive" personality? How have they helped or hurt you?

What activities or interests make you feel energized, fulfilled, or excited? Could any of these become a positive focus in your life?

_____

_____

_____

_____

_____

_____

_____

_____

_____

_____

_____

_____

Think about a time when you were deeply engaged in something constructive. What did it feel like, and how did it impact your mood or outlook?

What does "idle time" look like for you? How does it make you feel. and what could you do to use that time in a way that serves you?

What is one small, healthy obsession you could try this week? How will you approach it, and what steps can you take to stay consistent?

What fears or challenges do you have about replacing unhealthy habits with healthy ones? How could you address those fears?

How can you create balance so that even healthy
obsessions don't take over your life? What boundaries
or self-checks could help you stay grounded?

_____

_____

_____

_____

_____

_____

_____

_____

_____

_____

_____

_____

_____

If you could channel your energy into a cause, hobby, or skill, what would it be and why? How would this new focus change your life?

_____

_____

_____

_____

_____

_____

_____

_____

_____

_____

_____

_____

_____

_____

_____

Reflecting on these questions can help you understand your patterns, identify new passions, and move forward with purpose. Take your time, revisit these prompts as needed, and let your journal be a space for self-discovery and hope.

Tool #4 — Attitude of Gratitude

To be totally candid, I'm choosing to focus on this lesson for selfish reasons—this is something I need a lot of work on myself. Now, don't get it twisted; I am light-years ahead of where I was during my drinking days. But I still catch myself complaining too often, slipping into that "negative Nancy" mindset. (And to all the Nancy's out there reading this —you have every right to be a little ungrateful about how your name got dragged into this!)

Despite those moments, I've made massive strides in cultivating gratitude. I'm more aware now than ever that there's always something to be grateful for, no matter what. That doesn't mean life doesn't suck sometimes or that there aren't moments when you just need to vent. But here's the key: gratitude is a habit. When you make it a regular part of your life, it starts to shift your "stinkin' thinkin'" into an "attitude of gratitude." (Yep, I know—so clever, right?)

A simple mindset shift can make all the difference. Instead of saying, "I have to go to work today," say, "I get to go to work today." Instead of being frustrated about the mess your kids made, be grateful you have a home for them to make that mess in, and that you get to share it with them. Gratitude is not about pretending things aren't hard; it's about finding the silver lining, even when it takes some digging.

If you train your mind to look for the good, you'll start to see more of it. I firmly believe we can attract more of what we want by focusing on what we already have. Gratitude creates a shift in mindset that helps us notice opportunities, connect with others more deeply, and build resilience. This isn't just "surface level" stuff—it's a powerful tool that, once practiced regularly, can completely transform your outlook on life.

Practical Ways to Cultivate an Attitude of Gratitude

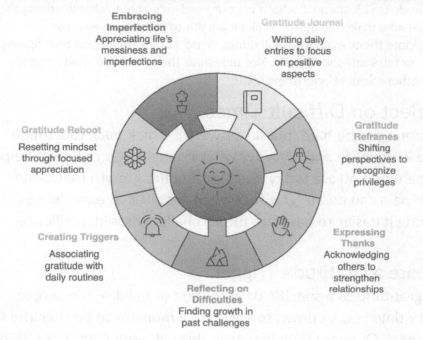

Embracing Imperfection
Appreciating life's messiness and imperfections

Gratitude Journal
Writing daily entries to focus on positive aspects

Gratitude Reboot
Resetting mindset through focused appreciation

Gratitude Reframes
Shifting perspectives to recognize privileges

Creating Triggers
Associating gratitude with daily routines

Expressing Thanks
Acknowledging others to strengthen relationships

Reflecting on Difficulties
Finding growth in past challenges

Start a Gratitude Journal

Keep a small notebook or use a notes app on your phone to write down three things you're grateful for every day. They don't have to be huge things—sometimes it's as simple as a sunny day, a good meal, or a kind word. This daily practice can reshape your focus and make you more attuned to the positive moments in your life.

Practice Gratitude "Reframes"

When you catch yourself complaining, pause and see if you can find a way to reframe it. Turn "I have to" into "I get to." This shift may seem small, but it's a way to recognize the hidden privileges in daily tasks. With time, reframing can become second nature, helping you see even tough moments in a new light.

Express Thanks to the People Around You

Gratitude isn't just about what's in your head—it's about acknowledging the people who make life better. Make it a habit to tell people when you appreciate them, even for small things. Send a quick thank-you text, leave a note, or tell someone directly. Not only does this spread positivity, but it strengthens your relationships too.

Reflect on Difficult Times

This one can be hard, but it's powerful. Think back to a tough time in your life and consider what it taught you or how it helped shape who you are today. Recognizing the growth that came from pain can create gratitude even for difficult experiences, making it easier to navigate future challenges with resilience.

Create a Gratitude Trigger

Tie gratitude to a specific daily routine or habit. For example, every time you sit down to eat, take a moment to be thankful for the meal. Or every time you walk through your front door, think of one thing you're grateful for that day. This helps make gratitude a regular part of your day without feeling forced.

Challenge Yourself to a "Gratitude Reboot"

If you're feeling especially down, do a "gratitude reboot"—take five minutes to think of everything you can appreciate at that moment. It might feel awkward or forced at first, but this concentrated burst of gratitude can reset your mindset and help you get through a tough day.

Embrace Imperfection

Gratitude doesn't require everything to be perfect; in fact, it's often most powerful when things aren't perfect. Life's messy moments have value, too. Embracing gratitude even when things are less than ideal helps you let go of unrealistic expectations and appreciate life as it is.

Turning Gratitude into a Habit

If you make gratitude a regular practice, it can be transformative. We can't control everything life throws at us, but we can choose how we respond. By focusing on what's good, even on tough days, we're training our minds to notice opportunities, stay resilient, and find joy in the everyday.

Gratitude may sound simple, but it's profound. It can shift your entire perspective, allowing you to appreciate the life you're living right now. The more you practice, the more you'll start to notice small blessings everywhere. And here's the beautiful thing: the more grateful you are for what you have, the more of what you need seems to find its way to you.

So make gratitude a habit. It might feel basic, but this practice has power far beyond what it may seem. Go back through this lesson if you need to, or come back to it whenever you feel yourself slipping. And remember: gratitude isn't a destination. It's a practice—a gift you can keep giving to yourself, every day.

Journaling Your Experience with "Attitude of Gratitude"

Gratitude has the power to reshape how you see the world, even during challenging times. Use your journal as a space to explore what gratitude means to you, how you've experienced it in your life, and where you might cultivate it further. Let yourself reflect honestly—not every day will feel overflowing with blessings, and that's okay. Gratitude is a practice, not perfection.

What are three things, big or small, that you're
grateful for right now? How do these things make your
life better?

_____

_____

_____

_____

_____

_____

_____

_____

_____

_____

_____

_____

Think back to a challenging time in your life. What lessons or growth came from that experience that you can feel grateful for today?

When you catch yourself feeling negative or complaining,
how might you reframe the situation to find something
to be thankful for? Write about one example.

_____

_____

_____

_____

_____

_____

_____

_____

_____

_____

_____

_____

_____

Who in your life has made a positive impact recently? How can you express your gratitude to them?

What's a simple, everyday moment—like enjoying a meal or seeing a sunset—that you often take for granted? How could you appreciate it more?

Have you ever experienced a "gratitude reboot" where you focused on everything good in your life? How did it feel. and could you try this again?

What imperfect or messy part of your life can you embrace with gratitude? How might shifting your perspective change how you feel about it?

_____

_____

_____

_____

_____

_____

_____

_____

_____

_____

_____

_____

_____

_____

_____

What is one small habit you could start today to cultivate gratitude regularly? How might this practice transform your outlook over time?

_____

_____

_____

_____

_____

_____

_____

_____

_____

_____

_____

_____

_____

_____

_____

_____

_____

Gratitude is a journey that unfolds as you practice it. These questions can guide you toward seeing the beauty in your life—even when it's hidden in the cracks—and help you build a habit that keeps on giving.

_____

Tool #5 Mindful Mindfulness

Wait, what? Mindful mindfulness? Isn't that a tautology—the opposite of an oxymoron? Yep, it absolutely is. But say it slowly and think about it for a moment.

Mindfulness itself requires mindful intention. In other words, we need to be deliberate about creating mindfulness in our lives. Habits don't just happen; they're trained. I know this from experience—I trained hard to become a habitual drinker. Back in high school, I wanted to fit in, so I worked tirelessly on finding and consuming alcohol because that's what I thought "cool" kids did. Now, I believe I was an addict from the start, but it still took work to build drinking into a habit. Just like I practiced being a drinker, I had to practice being mindful. The same goes for all of us—if we want mindfulness to become a daily part of our lives, it will take intention, repetition, and, well...mindfulness! That's just one part of what I mean by mindful mindfulness.

Mindfulness as Self-Observation
Another layer to mindful mindfulness is staying aware of where my mind actually is. For me, my brain can be a rough place if I don't guide it carefully. I can't control every thought that pops into my head, but I can control how I respond to those thoughts. This means I have to be mindful of how I'm reacting to intrusive or negative thoughts. If I notice an ugly thought creeping in, I have to catch myself and redirect back to my "attitude of gratitude" (yep, we're bringing that back). Without this awareness, my brain can easily spiral into a storm of negativity, and before I know it, I'm left with only depression, fear, and isolation. Mindful mindfulness means that when these thoughts arise, we don't just let them run wild. Instead, we observe them without judgment, and choose how to respond, rather than letting the thought dictate our mood or actions.

Mindfulness as Awareness of Surroundings

There's also an external aspect to mindfulness: being aware of what's happening around us. Where am I spending my time? Who am I spending it with? How am I treating the people who matter most to me? Am I present with them, or am I distracted, letting my mind drift off somewhere else? This kind of mindfulness helps us see how our actions impact others and ensures we're investing our energy in ways that truly align with our values.

All of this—mindfulness of our thoughts, our habits, and our environment—requires ongoing practice. It's like building any other habit; it needs repetition and, you guessed it, mindfulness to make it stick.

Practicing Mindful Mindfulness

- Set Daily Intentions
- Take a "Mindfulness Minute"
- Practice Responding, Not Reacting
- Scan Your Surroundings
- Incorporate Gratitude
- Reflect on Your Day

Set Daily Intentions

Start each day by setting a mindful intention. For example, "Today, I will be aware of my thoughts and redirect them when necessary" or "Today, I will be present with the people around me." Intentions give you a target to aim for, reminding you to bring mindfulness into each moment, even if it's just a little bit.

Take a "Mindfulness Minute"

Throughout the day, take quick breaks to check in with yourself. Pause, take a deep breath, and ask yourself, "Where is my mind right now? Am I focused on the present or lost in thought?" A few seconds of grounding can break negative thought loops and bring you back to the moment.

Practice Responding, Not Reacting

When a stressful or negative thought arises, try observing it without immediately reacting. This can feel tricky, but try to notice the thought as if you're watching it from the outside. Ask yourself, "Is this thought helpful?" If it's not, redirect your focus to something positive or neutral. Practicing this kind of mindfulness takes the power away from harmful thoughts.

Scan Your Surroundings

Take a few moments each day to mindfully look at your surroundings. Notice where you are, who you're with, and what's happening. Are you fully present? If not, gently bring your attention back to the people or the task in front of you. This simple practice builds a habit of awareness, helping you stay connected to the people and activities that matter most.

Incorporate Gratitude

Whenever you catch yourself caught up in a negative thought spiral, make a deliberate shift to gratitude. Think of one thing you're grateful for in that moment, however small it may be. This can help reset your focus, reminding you of what's going right, even when your thoughts are trying to pull you in the opposite direction.

Reflect on Your Day

At the end of each day, take a few moments to reflect on where your mind spent most of its time. Were you present? Did you respond to challenges thoughtfully? A daily reflection builds self-awareness, helping you notice patterns and make adjustments over time.

Why Mindful Mindfulness Matters

Mindful mindfulness keeps us grounded and gives us power over our own minds. It helps us navigate thoughts, emotions, and experiences without getting lost in them. When we're mindfully mindful, we're aware of our inner world and our outer world, giving ourselves the chance to respond with purpose, gratitude, and compassion.

We'll dive much deeper into this topic in its own dedicated lesson, but for now, remember this: mindfulness isn't just about sitting still and breathing deeply. It's about being fully present in your life, noticing where your attention goes, and making conscious choices to bring yourself back to what truly matters.

Journaling Your Experience with "Mindful Mindfulness"

Mindfulness isn't just about pausing your thoughts—it's about observing them, guiding them, and grounding yourself in the present moment. Use your journal to reflect on how mindfulness plays a role in your life now and how you'd like to cultivate it further. This is your space to explore your thoughts, behaviors, and surroundings with curiosity and without judgment.

When was the last time you felt fully present in the moment? What were you doing, and how did it feel?

What kinds of thoughts tend to distract or overwhelm
you? How do you currently respond when these
thoughts arise?

How could setting a daily intention help guide your thoughts and actions? Write an intention you'd like to practice tomorrow.

_____

_____

_____

_____

_____

_____

_____

_____

_____

_____

_____

_____

_____

Think about your surroundings—where you spend your time and who you spend it with. Are these aligned with your values and priorities? Why or why not?

When you're in a negative thought spiral, how might you use gratitude to ground yourself? What's one example of this you could try?

_____

_____

_____

_____

_____

_____

_____

_____

_____

_____

_____

_____

_____

_____

What does "responding instead of reacting" mean to you? Describe a time when you reacted impulsively and how you might approach it differently with mindfulness.

At the end of the day, how can reflecting on where your attention went help you become more mindful? What patterns do you notice in how you spend your mental energy?

_____

_____

_____

_____

_____

_____

_____

_____

_____

_____

_____

_____

_____

_____

_____

What small action could you take each day to remind yourself to stay present—such as a mindfulness minute or scanning your surroundings? How would this help you feel more grounded?

_____

_____

_____

_____

_____

_____

_____

_____

_____

_____

_____

_____

_____

_____

_____

By exploring these questions, you can begin to understand the patterns in your thoughts and actions, gently redirecting them toward the present moment and creating space for mindful growth.

Tool #6

K.I.N.D.
Kindness Is Now Deliberate

Helping others has been a huge part of my recovery journey and has genuinely made me a happier person. This is the foundation of A String of Hope, and now it's the entire mission behind Joy Academy. In my "humble opinion," I've always been a kind person. I care about people, and I feel deeply for those around me. I grew up in a church community where we practiced intentional acts of service, giving of ourselves to help others. That "servant's heart" mentality became second nature to me, rooted in the Golden Rule: "Do unto others as you would have them do unto you."

But when I got sober and started working through the 12 Steps, something really struck me about the last one:

Step #12: "Having had a spiritual awakening as the result of these steps, we tried to carry this message to alcoholics, and to practice these principles in all our affairs."

The step itself highlights "carrying the message," but what I've found is that the heart of Step Twelve goes beyond just helping others with addiction. It's about sharing what we've learned to make a positive impact in all areas of life, not just recovery. Through this journey, we start to transform into more compassionate, genuine, and empathetic people, and we get to extend that to everyone we meet.

This kindness becomes intentional, a way of being, because we know firsthand how meaningful it is to have someone care, especially during tough times. And honestly, we all have challenges, whether they're visible or not.

Why Kindness Needs to Be Deliberate

When kindness becomes a deliberate choice, it goes beyond just a nice gesture—it becomes part of our identity. In recovery, this kind of kindness can be a lifeline, and it has the power to create ripple effects in our communities. Making kindness a deliberate practice reminds us that we're not alone, that we're connected, and that there's always an opportunity to uplift others.

In a world where it's easy to be absorbed in our own struggles, choosing kindness as a daily practice takes courage and intentionality. Sometimes, it's about making that extra effort to really see people—to smile, to listen, to show empathy, even if they're strangers. And other times, it's about doing the harder work of being patient or forgiving in situations where it would be easier to walk away.

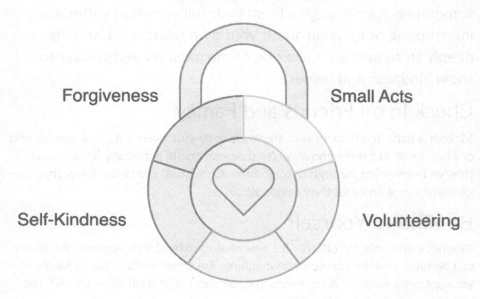

Deliberate Kindness

Forgiveness   Small Acts

Self-Kindness   Volunteering

Active Listening

Ways to Practice Deliberate Kindness (K.I.N.D.)

Look for Small Acts of Kindness Every Day

Not all acts of kindness have to be grand gestures. Start by holding the door open for someone, letting someone go ahead of you in line, or offering a compliment. These small acts might feel simple, but they add up and make people feel noticed and valued.

Volunteer Your Time

Whether it's a few hours at a local shelter, helping a neighbor with yard work, or even tutoring someone who needs a hand, volunteering is one of the most fulfilling ways to be kind. Helping others doesn't just benefit them; it also provides a sense of purpose and reminds you that you're capable of making a positive impact.

Practice Active Listening

Often, people just want someone to really listen to them. When someone is speaking, give them your full attention without interrupting or thinking about your own response. Listening deeply to someone can be one of the most powerful ways to show kindness and respect.

Check In on Friends and Family

Make it a habit to check in with those close to you, even if it's just a quick text or phone call. Let them know you're there for them, especially if you know they've been going through a tough time. Consistent check-ins show that you genuinely care and that they're not alone.

Be Kind to Yourself

Kindness isn't only for others—it's essential to extend it to yourself. Recovery can be hard, and life can be overwhelming. Take moments to speak kindly to yourself, give yourself grace when you fall short, and treat yourself with the same compassion you offer others.

Use Your Experiences to Help Others

One of the best ways to practice kindness is to share your journey openly and honestly with those who might need it. Be a mentor, offer support to someone facing similar struggles, or simply be someone who listens and understands. Your experience, especially your struggles, can be a source of strength and guidance for others.

Offer Forgiveness

Carrying resentment can be heavy, and offering forgiveness (to yourself or others) is a powerful act of kindness. Forgiving doesn't mean excusing wrongs—it means releasing yourself from the weight of resentment. In doing so, you free up more energy to pour into kindness.

Focus on the Impact, Not the Recognition

Practicing kindness is about lifting others, not about receiving praise or validation. When you do something kind, focus on the joy it brings to the other person, knowing that you're adding something positive to the world.

Why Deliberate Kindness Matters

When kindness becomes a choice—a deliberate act—it changes the way we relate to others and ourselves. Choosing to be kind, even in small ways, has a cumulative effect. It creates a sense of connectedness and resilience that can get us through life's toughest days. For those of us in recovery or navigating personal growth, kindness becomes a means of healing. We get to "carry the message" not only to others on the same path but to everyone we meet, spreading hope and compassion wherever we go.

In the end, deliberate kindness helps us become the people we're striving to be. It's a practice that enriches our lives, brings us closer to others, and reminds us of our shared humanity. So as you go through each day, remember that kindness isn't just a nice-to-have; it's a powerful, intentional practice that can make a real difference. Let's make kindness the kind of addiction that fuels our growth, connects us with others, and brings light to those around us.

Kindness, when practiced intentionally, has the power to transform not only the lives of others but also your own. Use your journal to reflect on how deliberate kindness shows up in your life. Consider how you can integrate it more deeply into your daily actions, relationships, and self-care. Your journal can help you uncover areas where kindness might be missing and where you can make a greater impact.

What's one small act of kindness you performed recently? How did it make you feel, and how do you think it impacted the other person?

Think of a time when someone showed you kindness during a tough moment. How did their action help you, and how can you pay it forward?

_____

_____

_____

_____

_____

_____

_____

_____

_____

_____

_____

_____

_____

_____

Are there areas in your life where you've struggled to extend kindness to yourself? What might it look like to treat yourself with the same compassion you offer others?

Who in your life might need a little extra kindness right now? How can you reach out to them in a way that feels meaningful?

Reflect on a moment when forgiveness—either for yourself or someone else—felt like an act of kindness. What did it change for you?

How can you incorporate deliberate kindness into your daily routine, like checking in with loved ones or being more patient with strangers?

What motivates you to be kind? How do your values, experiences, or challenges shape the way you practice kindness?

If you made kindness a daily habit, what impact do you think it would have on your relationships, your mindset, and your overall happiness?

Let these questions guide you toward making kindness a deliberate, life-enriching practice. Reflect often, and watch as even the smallest acts ripple outward in ways you may never fully realize.

Tool #7

The God of Your Understanding

After you read my story available at benfisherinspires.com you will know I was struggling with addiction while also leading worship at a church. When I played music, I felt so close to God, and I know I brought others closer, too. But at the same time, I was living outside the realm of authenticity, and that disconnect made it hard to truly understand God. It's one of the most difficult things for me to put into words, but I'm going to try.

When I joined Alcoholics Anonymous, I was introduced to the idea of a "God of my understanding." At that point, my relationship with the God I had previously known was, to put it lightly, rocky. I had felt betrayed by the church and had lost my sense of identity in the one thing that made me feel close to God. It was hard not to be resentful, to not think, If God is so powerful, why did He allow this to happen to me? And if He couldn't prevent it then, what makes me think He'll save me now?

But as I spent more time in the Big Book of A.A., I began to see things differently. I realized I had been confined by the beliefs and ideals of others. I was going through the motions, following a script that someone else had written for me. What I really needed was a deeply personal relationship with my higher power. That little word—my—changed everything. I began to understand that God wasn't some far-off superhero in the sky. Instead, God was within me, present and accessible.

Now, hear me out—I'm not saying I am God, not even close. What I'm saying is that God exists within each of us. Our separation from God often comes from the way we distance ourselves from our own truth, from living out of alignment with who we really are. To truly understand God, I had to dig deep to understand myself, and that meant being radically honest with myself.

The Journey to Your Own Understanding of God
This journey isn't about embracing someone else's idea of God. It's about discovering your own higher power—one that resonates with you personally. This concept may be uncomfortable at first, especially if you've had negative experiences with faith or religion. But coming to know your own understanding of God can bring a peace and sense of purpose that's truly grounding. And remember, it's okay if this journey is full of questions and uncertainty. That's often where the growth happens.

Journey to Understanding a Higher Power

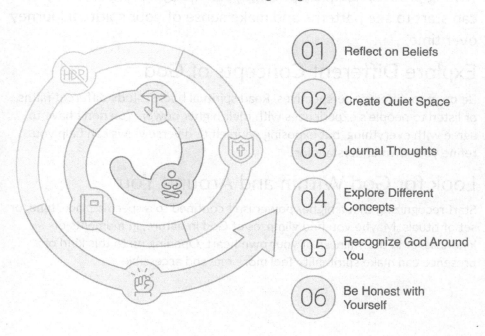

01 Reflect on Beliefs

02 Create Quiet Space

03 Journal Thoughts

04 Explore Different Concepts

05 Recognize God Around You

06 Be Honest with Yourself

How to Find the God of Your Understanding

Reflect on What You've Been Taught vs. What You Truly Feel

Start by considering the beliefs you were raised with, and compare them to what you truly feel in your heart. Ask yourself: Does this belief resonate with me? Why or why not? This process of exploration helps you separate inherited beliefs from the ones that hold true for you.

Create Space for Quiet Reflection

Finding a connection with your higher power requires time and space for introspection. Set aside a few minutes each day for quiet time. This might be through prayer, meditation, or simply sitting in silence. This allows you to tune out external influences and listen to what's inside.

Journal Your Journey

Write down any thoughts, feelings, or questions that come up during your time of reflection. Sometimes, clarity emerges in the writing process itself. By putting your thoughts into words, you can start to see patterns and make sense of your spiritual journey over time.

Explore Different Concepts of God

Be open to different perspectives. Read spiritual books, study different faiths, or listen to people's experiences with their higher power. You don't have to agree with everything, but exposing yourself to diverse views can help you refine your own understanding.

Look for God Within and Around You

Start recognizing that a higher power isn't confined to a specific place, time, or set of rituals. Maybe you find glimpses of God in nature, in moments of kindness, or in the stillness of your own heart. Opening up to this kind of presence can make spirituality feel more real and accessible.

Be Honest and Authentic with Yourself

True connection with a higher power requires honesty. Look within and ask yourself: What are my intentions? Am I living true to my values? This practice of self-reflection brings you closer to understanding God because it brings you closer to understanding yourself.

Let Go of Perfection

You don't have to "get it right" when it comes to understanding God. Spirituality isn't a destination; it's a journey. Allow yourself to ask questions and make mistakes. Trust that your relationship with your higher power will grow and evolve over time.

Trust in the Process

Trust that there is meaning in the journey, even if it feels uncertain. Building a relationship with a higher power isn't something that happens overnight. Give yourself grace and keep showing up.

Why This Understanding Matters

Connecting with the God of your understanding brings clarity, purpose, and resilience. In recovery, this relationship can provide a foundation that holds us steady, even on the hard days. It's not about conforming to someone else's idea of God but about discovering a higher power that feels true to you.

This journey has shown me that my understanding of God isn't rigid or distant—it's personal, present, and dynamic. I believe that God lives within us all, guiding us toward our truest, most authentic selves. And when we connect to that higher part of ourselves, we gain the strength to live with purpose, kindness, and love. So go ahead—ask the hard questions, explore freely, and let your heart guide you. You might just find that God is closer than you ever thought.

Journaling Your Experience with "The God of Your Understanding"

Exploring your connection with a higher power can be a deeply personal and transformative journey. Use your journal as a sacred space to reflect on your beliefs, experiences, and questions about spirituality. This is your opportunity to explore what feels authentic to you, without judgment or the need for perfection. Let your writing guide you closer to an understanding of God—or a higher power—that resonates with your truest self.

What beliefs about God or spirituality did you grow up with? How do those beliefs align or conflict with what you feel now?

When have you felt closest to a higher power or a sense of something greater than yourself? What was happening, and how did it make you feel?

What doubts or questions do you have about God or spirituality? How might exploring these questions bring you closer to your own understanding?

_____

_____

_____

_____

_____

_____

_____

_____

_____

_____

_____

_____

_____

_____

If you were to imagine a God or higher power that reflects your personal values and experiences, what would that look like? How would this presence make you feel?

What practices, like prayer, meditation, or time in nature, help you feel connected to something bigger than yourself? How could you incorporate these more often?

_____

_____

_____

_____

_____

_____

_____

_____

_____

_____

_____

_____

_____

_____

Think about a moment of kindness, beauty, or peace
that deeply moved you. How might that experience
reflect the presence of a higher power?

Are there areas of your life where you feel disconnected from your true self? How might reconnecting with a higher power help you find alignment and peace?

How does the idea of "the God of your understanding" encourage you to approach spirituality differently? What steps could you take to begin or deepen this journey?

_____

_____

_____

_____

_____

_____

_____

_____

_____

_____

_____

_____

_____

_____

_____

_____

_____

_____

_____

Let these questions guide you toward clarity and connection. This process is not about finding definitive answers but about embracing the journey of self-discovery and spiritual growth. Be patient, be curious, and trust that your path is uniquely your own.

Variable In = Variable Out

For as long as I can remember, my mom has told me, "If you fill your mind with garbage, you'll have a mind full of garbage." She'd say that whenever I was caught up watching a violent movie, playing video games, or blasting death metal (and, yes, I'm a sucker for music that sounds like a freight train crashing into another freight train at full speed). I used to shrug it off, thinking, "Okay, Mom, thanks, but I'm fine." It's funny how the older we get, the more we realize our parents were usually onto something.

In 2014, I was working for a plastics manufacturer and took a course on injection molding. The instructor said something that immediately brought me back to all those things my mom used to say: "Variable in equals variable out." He was talking about plastics, not life—but the message clicked for me. For those who don't know, producing a single plastic part involves a lot more precision than you'd think. Temperature, pressure, moisture, material type, press size, shape of the die... every tiny detail affects the outcome. Just one little variation can throw the whole process off.

At that time, I was deep in my alcoholism. I remember sitting in that class, thinking about grabbing my usual bottle of vodka right after work. At this particular drive-thru, they didn't even have to ask what I wanted. The second they saw my truck, they went straight for the cheap, nasty Kamchatka vodka. Day after day, I was literally filling myself with garbage. And as a result, my mind, my health, my relationships, and my whole life were becoming just as toxic. I was destroying myself from the inside out. Oddly enough, that plastics class brought it into focus for me: you can't keep filling yourself with the wrong stuff and expect anything good to come out. If you want things to get better, you have to start putting better things into the system.

Identifying and Taking Out the "Garbage"

So, what's your garbage? We all have something that weighs us down, holds us back, or leaves us feeling worse. Maybe it's the content you're consuming online, or a habit that's hurting more than helping. Maybe it's a toxic relationship. Whatever it is, the first step is recognizing it—and deciding that it's trash day. You've got to put it to the curb and leave it there.

This isn't easy. It can feel like you're giving up a piece of yourself or something that's familiar, but this is the first step toward making room for better things. Here are some ways to start the process and begin filling your life with better "variables":

Cycle of Positive Change

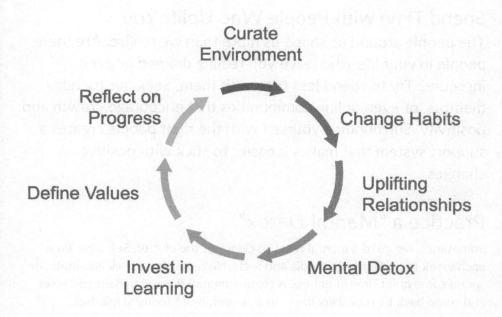

Practical Ways to Put in the Right "Variables"

Curate Your Environment

Look at what surrounds you daily—what you're watching, reading, and listening to. Social media can be a huge source of negativity, but you have the power to adjust your feed to focus on positivity, education, or inspiration. Consider unfollowing accounts or channels that bring you down and replacing them with ones that lift you up.

Change Your Habits, One at a Time

Big life changes start with small adjustments. Identify one habit that's dragging you down and replace it with something healthier. If you tend to scroll on your phone before bed, replace that time with a good book, meditation, or journaling. Small changes build momentum and can lead to significant transformation.

Spend Time with People Who Uplift You

The people around us shape us more than we realize. Are there people in your life who leave you feeling drained or even insecure? Try to spend less time with them. Seek out friends, mentors, or even online communities that encourage growth and positivity. Surrounding yourself with the right people creates a support system that makes it easier to stick with positive changes.

Practice a "Mental Detox"

Sometimes, we need a mental reset to clear out the clutter. Set aside time each week to unplug from media and technology. Go for a walk, meditate, or spend some quiet time in nature. A regular mental detox can help you reset and come back to your daily life with a clearer, more focused mindset.

Invest in Learning and Growth

Instead of filling time with activities that add no real value, commit to learning something new or developing a skill. This doesn't have to be complicated—pick up a book, take an online course, or work on a hobby. Investing in yourself not only boosts confidence but also opens up new opportunities.

Define and Pursue Your Values

Sometimes our "garbage" is filling our lives simply because we haven't defined what truly matters to us. Take time to reflect on your core values and ask yourself if your current lifestyle aligns with them. When you're clear on your values, it's easier to see what doesn't belong and to make choices that reflect who you want to be.

Reflect Regularly on Your Progress

Regular reflection helps keep you on track. Set aside time weekly or monthly to check in on how you're feeling, where your energy is going, and whether you're moving closer to the life you want. Use this time to adjust, let go of what's not working, and recommit to what is.

Why This Matters: Better In, Better Out

The truth is, you can't keep consuming toxic, negative, or shallow things and expect anything but the same in return. But when you start feeding yourself with what's good for you—mentally, emotionally, physically—the results start to show. Your mindset shifts, your relationships improve, your health gets better, and opportunities start appearing. The impact of these choices builds over time, creating a ripple effect in every area of your life.

So, take a look around: What are you putting in? What can you let go of to make room for what's better? This process isn't about perfection, and it's not about getting everything "right." It's about understanding that what you put into your mind, body, and soul affects what comes out—and choosing things that reflect the life you want to create.

Trust me, once you start making these changes, you'll notice a difference. Take out the garbage, put in the good stuff, and watch your life transform.

Journaling Your Experience with "Variable In = Variable Out"

Your choices—what you consume, who you surround yourself with, and how you spend your time—shape your life. Use your journal to reflect on the "garbage" you might need to let go of and the "good stuff" you want to replace it with. This process of self-awareness and intention can help you align your inputs with the outcomes you truly desire.

What "garbage" are you currently allowing into your life—whether it's habits, relationships, or content? How does it affect your mood, energy, or mindset?

When was the last time you intentionally consumed something uplifting. like a book. a podcast. or time with a positive person? How did it impact you?

What's one small habit you could replace with a healthier, more positive one? What steps can you take to start this change today?

_____

_____

_____

_____

_____

_____

_____

_____

_____

_____

_____

_____

_____

_____

Are there people in your life who drain your energy or leave you feeling worse? How might you create boundaries or spend less time in these relationships?

What kind of "mental detox" would help you clear out negativity and regain focus? How could you incorporate this regularly into your routine?

Think about your core values. Does your current lifestyle reflect what matters most to you? What could you shift to better align with those values?

What inspires you to grow—whether it's learning a skill, pursuing a passion, or spending time in nature? How can you prioritize more of this in your daily life?

How would your life change if you consistently focused on putting good things—positive habits, relationships, and content—into your mind and body? What would be different?

_____

_____

_____

_____

_____

_____

_____

_____

_____

_____

_____

_____

_____

_____

_____

These questions can help you identify areas of your life that need a reset and guide you toward making deliberate, empowering choices. Reflect often and adjust as you grow, knowing that each positive change builds toward a better future.

Tool #9 — Say Goodbye to the Victim Mentality

We've all been there. Life gets hard, and before we know it, we're stuck in a loop of "Why me?" or "Why does this always happen to me?" And let me tell you, I've played the role of victim more times than I'd like to admit. At my lowest points, it felt natural to slip into that mindset because it was easier than facing the reality of my own choices and responsibilities. But here's the harsh truth: as long as you're stuck in victim mode, you're giving away your power to change.

Victim mentality is a trap that keeps us focused on what's wrong instead of what we can do to make things right. It's a cycle of blaming circumstances, people, or even luck for where we are. And when we're focused on blame, there's no room for growth. We stay exactly where we are, never moving forward because we're waiting for something or someone else to make things better.

Letting go of the victim mentality doesn't mean pretending that bad things don't happen. It's not about ignoring real pain or pretending everything is fine. It's about choosing not to let those experiences define us or dictate our future. Life throws a lot at us, but we get to decide how we respond. The shift from "Why me?" to "What now?" is a powerful one, and it can change everything.

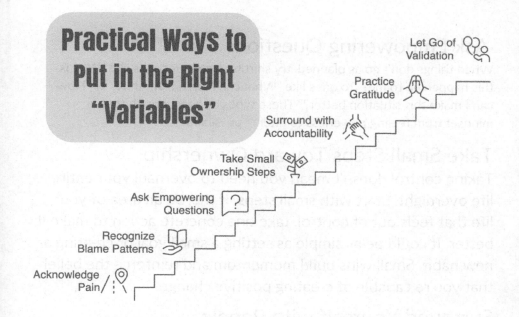

Practical Ways to Put in the Right "Variables"

- Let Go of Validation
- Practice Gratitude
- Surround with Accountability
- Take Small Ownership Steps
- Ask Empowering Questions
- Recognize Blame Patterns
- Acknowledge Pain

Acknowledge What Happened—Then Focus on What's Next

It's important to acknowledge any real pain or challenges you've faced. Don't push it down or pretend it didn't happen. But after you've acknowledged it, ask yourself, "What now?" Shift your focus from dwelling on the problem to finding a solution or a path forward. This doesn't mean everything will magically get better, but it allows you to take control of your actions moving forward.

Recognize Patterns of Blame and Excuses

Start paying attention to your thoughts and conversations. Are you quick to blame people or circumstances when things go wrong? Do you have a tendency to make excuses for why things aren't working out? Recognizing these patterns is the first step to changing them. Challenge yourself to own your part, even if it's uncomfortable.

Ask Empowering Questions

When things don't go as planned, try shifting from questions like "Why is this happening to me?" to ones like "What can I learn from this?" or "How can I make this situation better?" These types of questions shift your mindset from feeling powerless to finding possibilities.

Take Small Steps Toward Ownership

Taking control doesn't mean you need to overhaul your entire life overnight. Start with small steps. If there's an area of your life that feels out of control, take one concrete action to make it better. It could be as simple as setting a small goal or creating a new habit. Small wins build momentum and reinforce the belief that you're capable of creating positive change.

Surround Yourself with People Who Hold You Accountable

Being around people who uplift you and push you to be your best self can make a huge difference. Seek out people who encourage you to take responsibility rather than enabling a victim mindset. These people will help you see the bigger picture and remind you of your strength when you need it most.

Practice Gratitude for Your Strengths and Growth

When we're in victim mode, we tend to overlook our strengths and focus on our weaknesses. Make a habit of acknowledging what you're doing well. Recognize your own resilience, the lessons you've learned, and the ways you've grown. Practicing gratitude for your own progress can shift your perspective and give you a sense of agency.

Let Go of the Need for Validation

The victim mentality often comes with a craving for sympathy and validation. If you find yourself sharing your struggles mainly to get people to feel sorry for you, try to shift that pattern. Seek out encouragement and support, yes, but not as a way to reinforce the belief that you're helpless. Use connection as a source of motivation, not as a validation for staying stuck.

Embracing Accountability and Taking Your Power Back

Choosing to leave the victim mentality behind is about reclaiming your power. When you're no longer waiting for things to get better on their own, you realize that you have the strength to create the life you want, one choice at a time. Accountability doesn't mean you'll never struggle or face setbacks, but it does mean that you're choosing to move forward with purpose, not excuses.

This mindset shift isn't always easy, and you'll probably catch yourself slipping back into old habits from time to time. That's okay. The goal is progress, not perfection. The more you practice taking ownership, the more natural it becomes.

So, when life throws you curveballs, don't ask, "Why me?" Instead, ask, "What's next?" Embrace the power of choice, and remember that you're stronger than your circumstances. Let's take that power back.

Journaling Your Experience with "Say Goodbye to the Victim Mentality"

Breaking free from the victim mentality is about reclaiming your power to shape your life. Use your journal to explore the thoughts, habits, or patterns that may be holding you back, and reflect on how you can shift your mindset from blame to action. Writing honestly about your experiences can help you uncover the strength and resilience you already have within you.

Think about a time when you felt like a victim of your circumstances. How did staying in that mindset affect your actions, mood, or relationships?

What's one small, concrete action you can take today to start regaining control in an area of your life? How will this step make you feel?

When challenges arise, how can you reframe "Why is this happening to me?" into "What can I learn from this?" or "What's next?" Write about a recent situation where this shift could have helped.

_____

_____

_____

_____

_____

_____

_____

_____

_____

_____

_____

_____

_____

_____

Who in your life holds you accountable and encourages you to grow? How can you spend more time with them or seek out similar relationships?

What strengths, skills, or qualities do you have that help
you overcome challenges? How can focusing on these
strengths help you move forward?

_____

_____

_____

_____

_____

_____

_____

_____

_____

_____

_____

_____

_____

Is there an area where you're seeking validation through sympathy? How might you shift toward seeking encouragement or motivation instead?

What "garbage" are you currently allowing into your life—
whether it's habits, relationships, or content? How does it
affect your mood, energy, or mindset?

Imagine your life one year from now if you fully embraced accountability and ownership of your choices. What would be different, and how would it feel?

These questions are designed to help you step out of the "Why me?" mindset and into a place of empowerment. Reflect often, celebrate your progress, and keep taking steps toward reclaiming your power.

Made in the USA
Las Vegas, NV
13 December 2024

14054435R00066